BLACK PETER

THE RED-HEADED LEAGUE

SIR ARTHUR CONAN DOYLE

BLACK PETER
THE RED-HEADED LEAGUE

Edited by Erik Hvid
Revised edition 1995 by Erik Hvid
Illustrations by Pawel Marczak

The vocabulary is based on
Michael West: A General Service List of
English Words, revised & enlarged edition, 1953
Pacemaker Core Vocabulary, 1975
Salling/Hvid: English-Danish Basic Dictionary, 1970
J. A. van Ek: The Threshold Level for Modern Language
Learning in Schools, 1976

Series editors: Ulla Malmmose
and Charlotte Bistrup

Cover Layout & Silhouette: Mette Plesner
Cover Photo: iStockphoto/Peeter Viisimaa RF

© 1980 EASY READERS, Copenhagen
- a subsidiary of Lindhardt og Ringhof Forlag A/S,
an Egmont company.
ISBN Denmark 978-87-23-50603-0
www.easyreaders.eu

The CEFR levels stated on the back of the book
are approximate levels.

Easy Readers

EGMONT

Printed in Denmark

SIR ARTHUR CONAN DOYLE
(1859–1930)

studied medicine at Edinburgh University and practised for some years as a doctor. He served in the British Army in South Africa during the Boer War.

Conan Doyle is famous for his creation of Sherlock Holmes, the amateur detective, and his friend, Dr. Watson, who both appear in *The Adventures of Sherlock Holmes* (1891) and *The Memoirs of Sherlock Holmes* (1894). He also wrote a book about the Boer War, a play *Story of Waterloo* and a series of historical romances. In his later years he became interested in spiritualism and wrote *The History of Spiritualism*.

Sherlock Holmes appears to us as a rather eccentric man, peculiar in his behaviour and with unusual gifts. His qualities are set off by the fact that we always see him on the background of Dr. Watson, who was a very poor detective.

The Adventures of Sherlock Holmes was a great success. Conan Doyle tired of his hero, however, but when he tried killing him off to get rid of him for ever, the indignation of his public forced him to bring him back to life.

The stories about Sherlock Holmes belong to the so-called literature of entertainment, of which Conan Doyle was a master.

Contents

Black Peter 9

The Red-Headed League 53

Black Peter

1.

My friend had never been in better form than he was in the year '95. He was then famous, and among his *clients* were many well-known people. Holmes, however, lived for his work, and except in the case of the Duke of Holdernesse he has never claimed any large amount of money for his help. He often refused his help to the powerful and rich where he had no interest in the problem, while he could work hard for weeks with the problems of some poor client whose case offered those strange qualities which he liked so much.

During the first week of July my friend had been away so often and so long from our house that I knew he had something on his hand. The fact that several men called during that time and asked for Captain Basil made me understand that Holmes was working somewhere under one of the *disguises* and names which he used when he did not want to be recognized. He said nothing of his business to me and I did not ask him about it. The first sign which he gave me of the case he was working on was a strange one. He had gone out before breakfast, and I had sat down to mine, when he walked into the room, his hat upon his head, and a long *spear*, which he held under his arm.

clients, the people who came to him for help
disguise, other clothes, another hat etc. so that people could not see who he was

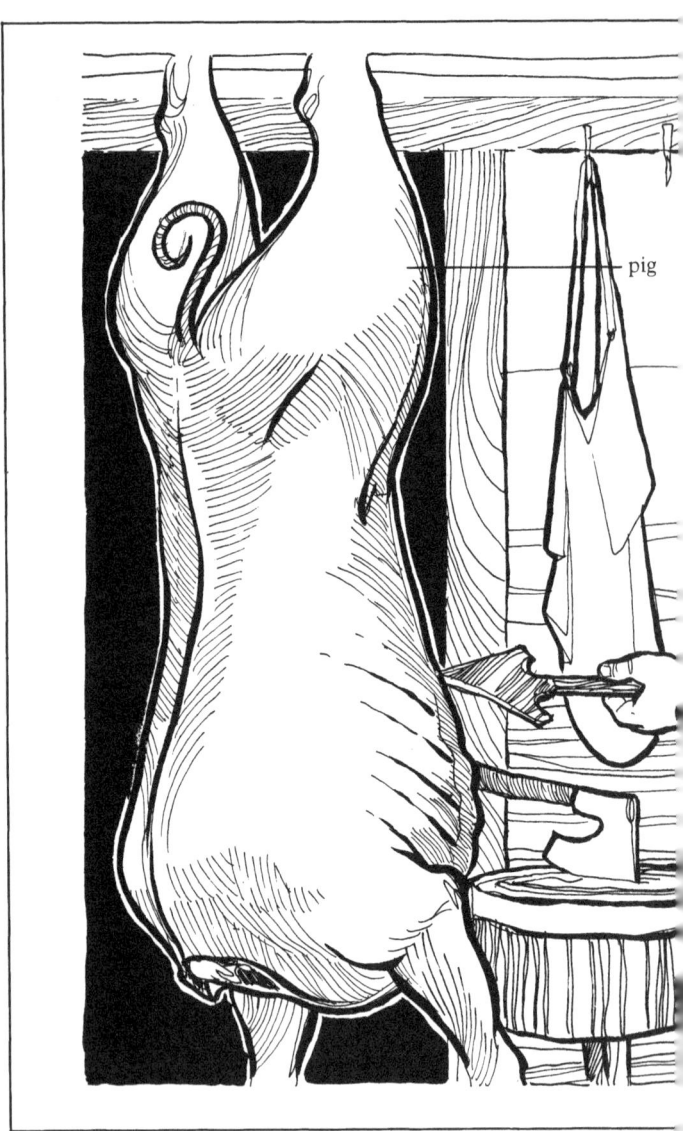

"But my dear Holmes!" I cried. "You don't mean to say that you have been walking about London with that thing?"

"I went to the *butcher*'s and back."

"The butcher's?"

"And I return with a very good *appetite*. There can be no question, my dear Watson, of the value of *exercise* before breakfast. But I am sure that you will not guess the form that my exercise has taken."

"I will not attempt it."

He laughed and sat down at the table.

"If you had looked into the butcher's back shop you would have seen a dead *pig* hanging from the *ceiling* and a gentleman trying to run his spear through it. I was that gentleman, and I have made sure that even if I use all my strength, I cannot run my spear through the pig with a single blow. Perhaps you would care to try?"

"Not for worlds. But why were you doing this?"

"Because it seemed to me that it would be of interest for the *mystery* of Woodman's Lee. Ah, Hopkins, I got your letter and I have been expecting you. Come and sit down."

I at once recognized our *visitor* as Stanley Hopkins, a young *policeman* Holmes had often talked about. He sat down looking very sad and troubled.

"No, thank you, sir. I had breakfast before I came

---

butcher, man who kills animals for food
appetite, if you can eat much you have a good appetite
exercise, walking and running is good exercise
pig, ceiling: see picture on page 10–11
mystery, something which is difficult or impossible to understand
visitor, person who visits

round. I spent the night in town, for I came up yesterday to *report*."

"And what had you to report?"

"*Failure*, sir – complete failure."

"You have made no progress?"

"None."

"Dear me! I must have a look at the matter."

"I wish to heavens that you would, Mr. Holmes. It is

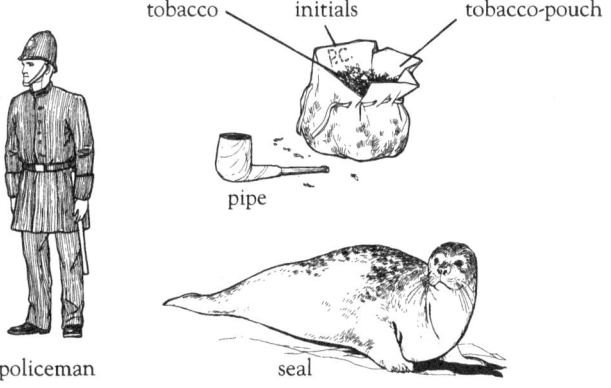

my first big chance, and I don't know what to do. Please come down and lend me a hand."

"Well, well, it happens that I have already read the report. By the way, what do you make of that *tobacco-pouch* which was found in the house? Doesn't that help you?"

Hopkins looked surprised.

"It was the man's own pouch, sir. His *initials* were in

report, say what had happened and what he had found out
failure, not success

it. And it was of *sealskin* – and he was an old *sealer*."

"But he had no *pipe*."

sealskin

whale

the sealer SEA UNICORN

"No, sir, we could find no pipe; indeed, he smoked very little. And yet he might have kept some tobacco for his friends."

"No doubt. I only mention it because if I had had the case, I think that I should have made that the starting-point of my *investigation*. However, my friend, Dr. Watson, knows nothing of this matter and I shouldn't mind hearing again what happened; just tell us in a few words what it is all about."

Stanley Hopkins took a piece of paper from his pocket.

"I have a few things here about the dead man, Captain Peter Carey. He was born in '45 – fifty years old. He was a most successful seal and *whale* fisher. In 1883 he

> *sealer*, man who kills seals to get the skin; ship from which seals are caught
> *pipe*: see picture on page 13
> *his investigation*, his work to find out who had killed the man

commanded the sealer SEA UNICORN, of *Dundee*. He had then had great success for some years, and in the following year, 1884, he gave up *sealing*. After that he travelled for some years, and then he bought a small place called Woodman's Lee, near Forest Row, in *Sussex*. There he has lived for six years, and there he died just a week ago today."

"There were some very *unusual* points about the man. He was always silent, one had a feeling that he had something on his mind, something he couldn't forget. In the house lived his wife, his daughter, twenty years

---

sealing, catching seals
unususal, strange or surprising; points that made him different from other men

old, and two women-*servants*. The man was a *drunkard*, and people have seen him drive his wife and daughter out of doors in the middle of the night and beat them until someone stopped him. In short, Mr. Holmes, you would go far before you found a man who was worse than Peter Carey, and I have heard that he was no better when he commanded his ship. He was known among the sealers as Black Peter, and they had given him that name not only because of his dark skin and the colour of his long *beard*, but because they were very much afraid of him. I need not say that the sealers *hated* him, and that I have heard no one say that it made him sad to hear that he had been killed."

"You must have read in the reports about the man's *cabin*, Mr. Holmes; but perhaps your friend here has not heard of it. He had built himself a small house of wood in the garden – he always called it "the cabin" – a few hundred yards from his house, and it was here that he slept every night. It was a small house with only one room, sixteen *feet* by ten. He kept the *key* in his pocket,

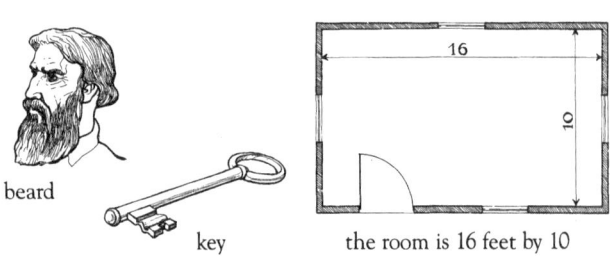

beard   key   the room is 16 feet by 10

servant, someone who works in a house for money
drunkard, person who drinks too much
hate, not like
cabin, room in a ship where you sleep
one foot = 30.48 centimetres

made his own bed, cleaned it himself and allowed no other person to enter it. There are small windows on each side, which were covered by *curtains*, and never opened. One of these windows was facing the road, and when the light burned in it at night, people would point it out to each other and wonder what Black Peter was doing in there."

"You remember that a man called Slater, walking from Forest Row about one o'clock in the morning – two days before the *murder* – stopped as he passed the garden and looked at the light still shining among the trees. He is sure that the *shadow* of a man's head was clearly seen on the curtain, and that this shadow was certainly not the shadow of Peter Carey's head. He knew Peter Carey well. It was the shadow of a man with a beard, but the beard was short and came forwards in a way very different from the captain's. So he says, but he had been two hours in the *public-house* and it is some distance from the road to the window. And this was Monday, and the man was murdered upon the Wednesday."

"On the Tuesday Peter Carey was red in his face with drink and wild as a wild animal. Late in the evening he went down to his cabin. About two o'clock the following morning his daughter, who slept with her window open, heard a wild *yell* from the cabin, but it was no unusual thing for him to shout when he was in drink, so nobody took any notice. At seven the girls got up, and one of them saw that the door of the cabin was open, but

curtain, shadow: see picture on page 18
murder, killing of another person
public-house, if you want something to drink, you go to the publichouse (= the pub)
yell, loud, sharp cry

everybody was so much afraid of the man that it was about 12 o'clock before anyone went down to see what had become of him. Looking in at the open door they saw a sight that sent them flying with white faces into the village. Within an hour I was on the spot."

"Well, Mr. Holmes, I give you my word that I got a shake when I put my head into that little house. There were thousands of *flies* and the walls and the floor were

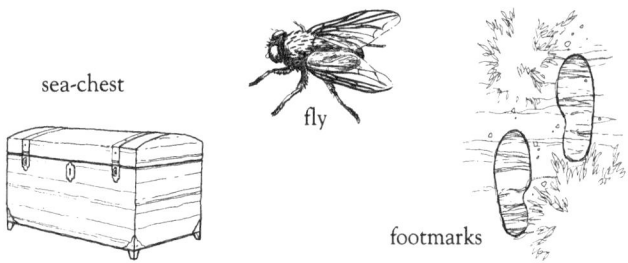

sea-chest

fly

footmarks

like a *slaughter-house*. He had called it a cabin, and a cabin it was, sure enough, for you would think that you were in a ship. There was a *bunk* at one end, a *sea-chest*, *charts*, a picture of the SEA UNICORN, a line of *log-books* on a *shelf*, all as you would expect to find it in a captain's room. And there in the middle of it was the man himself, a *harpoon* run through him and deep into the wood of the wall behind him. Of course, he was quite dead, and he had been so from the moment he gave out that last yell."

"I know how you work, sir, so before I allowed anybody to take anything away, I *examined* with great care the ground outside, and also the floor of the room. There were no *footmarks*."

---

slaughter-house, place where animals are killed for food
bunk, a bed in a ships cabin
chart, log-book, shelf, harpoon: see picture on page 20
log-book, book in which the captain writes every day where the ship is, how fast it goes, how the weather is etc.
examine, look at very carefully

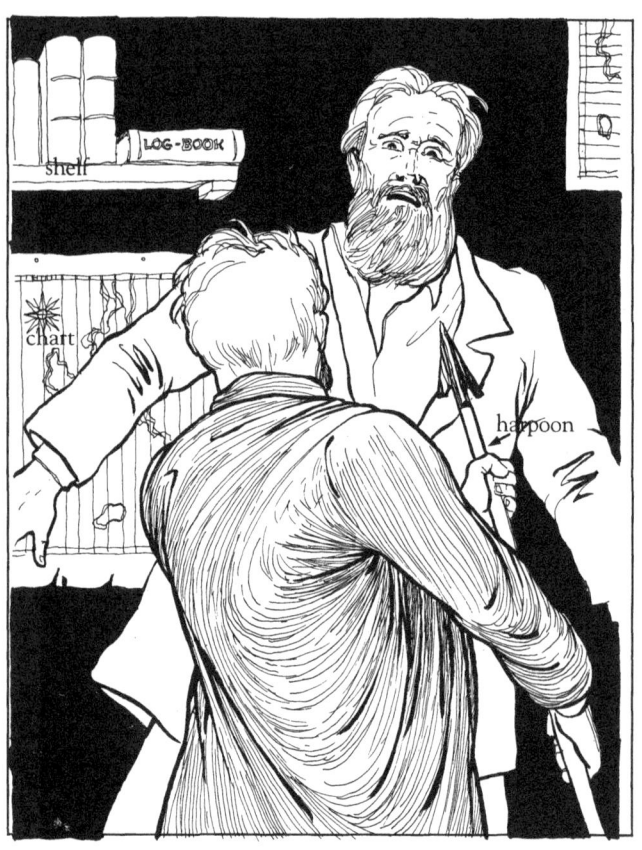

"You mean that you saw no footmarks?"

"I'm sure, sir, that there were none."

"My good Hopkins, I have *investigated* many *crimes*, but I have never yet seen one where there were no foot-marks or other marks, and it cannot be right that there

> *investigate*, try to find out what has happened
> *crime*, murder is a crime

are no marks in this room which can help us. I understand, however, from the report that you did notice some objects of interest!"

"I was a fool not to call you in at the time, Mr. Holmes. However, that's too late now. Yes, there were several interesting objects in the room. One was the harpoon with which the man was killed. It had been hanging on the wall, where there were two more. On all three harpoons were the name SEA UNICORN. This shows us that the *murderer* took the first *weapon* that came in his way. The fact that Peter Carey was killed at two in the morning, and that he was fully dressed suggests that he knew the man was coming. Also, there was a *bottle* of rum and two glasses on the table."

"Yes," said Holmes; "I think that you are right. Were there any other strong drinks in the room?"

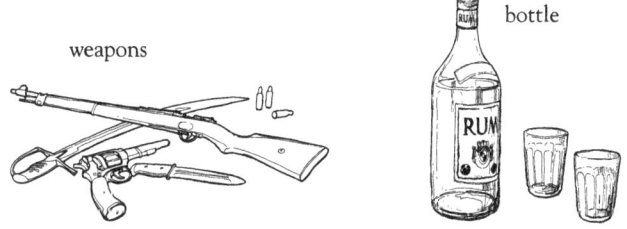

"Yes. There was some brandy and whisky on the seachest. It is of no importance to us, however, since the bottles were full and had therefore not been used."

"Everything in the room is of some importance," said Holmes. "However, let us hear some more of the objects

| *the murderer*, the man who killed Peter Carey

which you think are of interest in the case."

"There was this tobacco-pouch on the table."

"What part of the table?"

"It lay in the middle. It was of sealskin, with the letters P.C. There was a little tobacco in it, strong ship's tobacco."

"Good! What more?"

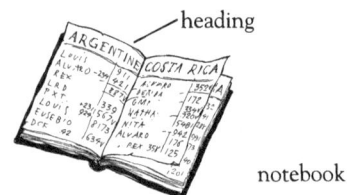

notebook

Stanley Hopkins took from his pocket a *notebook*. On the first page were written the initials. "J.H.N." and the year "1883". Holmes laid it on the table and examined it while Hopkins and I looked over each shoulder. On the second page were the letters "C.P.R." and then came several pages with numbers. Another *heading* was Argentine, another Costa Rica, and another Sao Paulo, each with pages of signs and numbers after it.

"What do you think of these?" asked Holmes.

"They are lists of *Stock Exchange securities*. I thought that J.H.N. were the initials of a *broker*, and that C.P.R. may have been his client."

> *stock*, paper saying how much money a man has placed in a business company
> *Stock Exchange*, place where people can buy and sell stocks
> *security*, paper with the numbers of some stocks and the name of the owner of the stocks
> *broker*, man whose business it is to buy and sell stocks for his clients

"Try Canadian Pacific Railway," said Holmes.

"What a fool I have been," cried Hopkins. "Of course it is as you say. Then J.H.N. are the only initials we have to find out. I have already examined the old Stock Exchange lists, and I can find no one in 1883 whose initials are J.H.N. But I feel that these initials are very important. You will admit, Mr. Holmes, that it is possible that they are the initials of the second person who was present – in other words the murderer. I would also say that the fact that there is this list of securities in the case gives us for the first time an idea of why Peter Carey was killed."

Sherlock Holmes' face showed that he was surprised to hear about the notebook.

"I must admit both your points," said he. "I must say that the notebook, which did not appear in the report, changes any views which I may have formed. I had come to a *theory* of the crime in which I can find no place for this. Have you tried to find any of the securities here mentioned?"

"Yes, But I'm afraid that the complete list of the *stock-holders* is in South America, and that it will take us some weeks to find them."

Holmes had been examining the notebook with his *magnifying lens*.

"Yes, sir, it is a blood-*stain*. I told you that I found it on the floor."

"What side was the blood on?"

---

theory, an idea of how everything had happened
stock-holder, owner of stocks
magnifying lens: see picture on page 24
stain, the blood on the notebook had left a mark

"On the side next to the floor."

"Which proves, of course, that the book was dropped after the man was murdered."

"Yes, Mr. Holmes. I noticed that point, and I guessed that it was dropped by the murderer when he left. It lay near the door."

"I suppose that none of these securities were found

among the dead man's things?"

"No, sir."

"Have you any reason to think that Peter Carey was *robbed*?"

"No, sir. Nothing seemed to have been touched."

"Dear me, it is certainly a very interesting case. Then there was a *knife*, was there not?"

"A *sheath*-knife, still in its sheath. It lay at the feet of the dead man. Mrs. Carey says that it was her husband's knife."

Holmes was silent for some time.

"Well," said he at last, "I suppose that I shall have to come out and have a look at it."

Stanley Hopkins gave a cry of pleasure.

"Thank you, sir. That will indeed be a weight off my mind."

"All right. But it would have been easier a week ago," said he. "But even now my visit may be useful. Watson, if you can come with me, I should be very glad of your company. If you will call a *four-wheeler*, Hopkins, we shall be ready to start for Forest Row in a quarter of an hour."

knife   sheath

rob, take things of great value that belong to someone else, for example money from a bank
four-wheeler: see picture on page 26

four-wheeler

2.

We got off the train at a small station and drove for some miles through a wood. Here in an open place on the green side of a hill stood a long, low stone house, at some distance from the road. Nearer the road, with *bushes* on

three sides, was a small out-house, one window and the door facing the road. It was the scene of the murder.

We went first to the house where a tired-looking, grey-haired woman, the *widow* of the murdered man, *answered our ring*. Her face and the look in her eyes told of the hard time she had had with her husband. With her was her daughter, a *pale* girl, who told us she was glad her father was dead and that she *blessed* the man who killed him.

The outhouse was the simplest of houses, with walls of wood, one window beside the door and one on the farther side. Stanley Hopkins took the key from his pocket and was going to open the door, when he stopped with a look of surprise on his face.

"Someone has tried to get in," he said.

There could be no doubt of the fact. Someone had cut the wood with a knife, and it was clear that it had been done a very short time ago. Holmes was examining the window.

"Someone has tried to open this also. Whoever it was has failed to make his way in. He must have been a very poor *burglar*."

"This is a very surprising thing," said Hopkins; "I am sure that these marks were not here yesterday evening."

"Someone from the village, perhaps," I suggested.

"No, I don't think so. Few of them would dare to set foot here, and none of them would dare to force their way

---

widow, woman whose husband has died
answered our ring, opened the door when we rang the bell
pale, (of a person's face) having little colour
bless someone, wish that he will be happy
burglar, person who breaks into a house to steal

into the cabin. What do you think of it, Mr. Holmes?"

"I think that when he came, he expected to find the door open. He tried to get in with the *blade* of a very small *penknife*. He couldn't. What would he do?"

"Come again next night with a better *tool*."

"So I should say. And we must be there to receive him. But let us go into the cabin now."

The dead body had been taken away, but the *furniture* of the little room still stood as it had been on the night of the crime. For two hours Holmes examined every object in the room, but his face showed that he found nothing of interest. He stopped only once.

"Have you taken anything off this shelf, Hopkins?"

"No, I have moved nothing."

"You can see that something has been taken. There is less dust in this corner of the shelf. It may have been a book lying on its side. It may have been a box. Well, well, I can do nothing more. Let us walk in these beautiful woods, Watson, and give a few hours to the birds and the flowers. We shall meet you here later, Hopkins, and see if we can meet the gentleman who has paid this visit in the night."

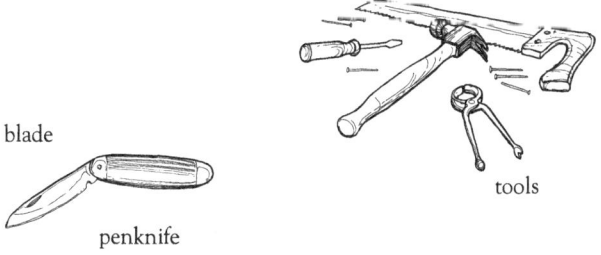

| *furniture*, chairs, tables and beds are pieces of furniture

3.

It was past eleven when we met again at the cabin. Hopkins wanted to leave the door of the cabin open, but Holmes said that this would make the man think that something was wrong, and that the door could be opened with a strong blade. He also suggested that we should wait, not in the cabin, but outside among the bushes which were round the farther window. In this way we should be able to watch our man if he struck a light, and see what he wanted in the cabin.

We sat down among the bushes, waiting for what might come. At first we heard the steps of a few men from the village or the sound of their voices, but soon everything was still. A fine rain was falling.

It was half past two when we heard a sound from the direction of the road. Someone had entered the garden. Again there was a long *silence*, and then a step was heard on the other side of the house and a moment later the sound of someone working with a knife. The man was trying to open the door! This time his tool was better, for we heard the door open. Then a *match* was struck, and the next moment the light from a *candle* filled the cabin. Through the curtains we watched the scene.

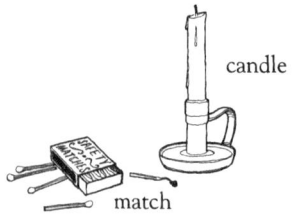

| *silence*, there were no sounds

The visitor was a young man, thin and very pale, with a black *moustache*. He could not have been much above twenty years of age, and he was dressed like a gentleman. He looked round. Then he put the candle on the table and moved into one of the corners, where we could not see him. He returned with a large book, one of the log-books from the shelves. He leaned on the table and

moustache

quickly turned over the *leaves* of this book until he found what he was looking for. Then, he closed the book, put it back in the corner and put out the light. He had hardly turned to leave the house when Hopkins' hand was on his shoulder and I heard him cry out in *terror* when he understood that he was taken. Hopkins lit the candle again, and there was our man, shaking all over. He sat down on the sea-chest, and looked from one of us to the other.

"Now, my fine fellow, who are you, and what do you want here?"

The man pulled himself together.

"You are *detectives*, I suppose?" said he. "You think that

---

leaf (two *leaves*), a leaf = 2 pages in a book
terror, great fear
detective, person, often a policeman, whose job it is to find and catch people who have for example stolen something or killed someone

I have something to do with the death of Peter Carey. I tell you that I did not kill him."

"We'll see about that," said Hopkins. "First of all, what is your name?"

"It is John Hopley Neligan."

I saw that Holmes and Hopkins looked at each other.

"What are you doing here?"

"Why should I tell you?"

"If you have no answer it may be very bad for you."

"Well, I will tell you," he said. "Why should I not? Did you ever hear of Dawson & Neligan?"

I could see from Hopkins' face that he never had; but Holmes was interested.

"You mean the West Country *bankers*," said he. "They failed for a million, half the families of Cornwall lost their money and Neligan *disappeared*."

"Yes. Neligan was my father."

At last we were getting something we could use, and yet it seemed impossible to explain what a disappeared banker had to do with Peter Carey with one of his own harpoons run through him and deep into the wall. We all listened with great interest to the young man's words.

"It was my father who *was* really *concerned*. Dawson was an old man and did not work in the bank any more. I was only ten years of age at the time, but I was old enough to feel that a very bad thing had happened. People have always said that my father stole all the securities and took them away with him when he left. It is not true. He believed that if they would give him

banker, person who owns a bank
disappeared, went away and was never seen again
was concerned, what happened was important to him

yacht

time in which to sell them, he would be able to pay everybody what they had lost. He started in his little *yacht* for Norway, and I can remember that last night when he said good-bye to my mother. He left us a list of the securities he was taking, and he said that he would come back soon and that no one who had placed money in his bank would lose it. Well, no word was ever heard of him again. Both the yacht and he disappeared. We believed, my mother and I, that he and it were at the *bottom* of the sea. We had a good friend, however, who is a business man, and it was he who discovered some time ago that someone had tried to sell the securities that my father had taken with him on the London market. We were surprised, of course. For many months I tried to find the man, and at last, after many difficulties, I discovered that he had been Captain Peter Carey, the owner of this house."

"Of course I tried to find out who the man was. I found that he had been in command of a sealer which was to return from the Arctic Seas at the very time when my father was crossing to Norway, in August. There were many storms that year, and my father's yacht may well have been blown to the north and there met Captain Peter Carey's ship. If that were so, what had become of my father? In any case, if I could get Peter Carey to tell me how these securities came on the market, I could prove that my father had not sold them, and that he did not think of himself when he took them."

"I came down here to see the captain, but it was at this moment that he was murdered. I read in a newspaper about his cabin and that the old logbooks of his ship were in it. I thought that if I could see what happened in the month of August 1883, on the SEA UNICORN, I might be able to find out what had happened to my father. I tried last night to get at these log-books, but could not open the door. Tonight I tried again, and succeeded; but I find that the pages which deal with that month have been taken out of the book. It was at that moment you came."

| *bottom*, bed of the sea, of a lake, a river etc.

"Is that all?" asked Hopkins.

"Yes, that's all." He looked away as he said it.

"You have nothing else to tell us?"

"No, there is nothing."

"Then how will you explain that we found this in the cabin?" cried Hopkins as he held up the notebook with the initials of the man on the first leaf and the bloodstain.

"Where did you get it?" he said. "I did not know. I thought I had lost it at the hotel."

"That's enough," said Hopkins. "What else you have to tell you must tell the police. You will walk with me now to the police-station. Well, Mr. Holmes, I thank you and your friend very much for coming down to help me. I see now that it was not necessary, but I am very glad that you came. There are rooms for you at the Brambletye Hotel, so we can all walk down to the village together."

4.

"Well, Watson, what do you think of it?" asked Holmes as we travelled back next morning.

"I can see that you are not satisfied."

"Oh, yes, my dear Watson, I am perfectly satisfied. But I had hoped for better things from Stanley Hopkins. One should always look for a possible *alternative*."

"What, then, is the alternative?"

"That is the line I have followed. It may give nothing. I cannot tell. But I shall follow it to the end."

Several letters were waiting for Holmes at Baker Street. He took one of them, opened it, and began to laugh.

"Excellent, Watson. The alternative develops. Just write two *telegrams* for me: "Sumner, *Shipping Agent*,

Ratcliff Highway. Send three men on, to arrive at ten tomorrow morning. – Basil." That's my name in those *parts*. The other is "Inspector Stanley Hopkins, 46 Lord Street, Brixton. Come breakfast tomorrow at nine-thirty. Important. – Sherlock Holmes." There, Watson, I have

---

alternative, another way to explain what has happened. Hopkins thinks that Neligan killed Peter Carey; the alternative is that it was someone else
shipping agent, man who helps the owner of a ship to find seamen
parts, people in that district knew him as Basil

thought of nothing but this case for ten days. I'm sure that tomorrow we shall hear the last of it for ever."

At nine-thirty the next morning Inspector Stanley Hopkins appeared, and we sat down together to a very good breakfast, which Mrs. Hudson had prepared. The young detective was very pleased with his success.

"You really think that you have found the right man?" asked Holmes.

"I could not think of a more complete case."

"It didn't seem so clear to me."

"You surprise me, Mr. Holmes. What more could one ask for?"

"Are you able to explain every point?"

"Certainly. I find that young Neligan arrived at the Brambletye Hotel on the very day of the crime. He came, he said, to play *golf*. His room was on the ground floor,

He came, he said, to play golf

and he could get out when he liked. That very night he went down to Woodman's Lee, saw Peter Carey at the cabin, *quarrelled* with him, and killed him with the harpoon. Then he ran out of the cabin, dropping the notebook which he had brought with him to question Peter Carey about the securities. You may have noticed

| *quarelled*, they used bad language at each other

that some of them were marked with *ticks* and the others – most of them – were not. Those which are ticked are the ones which someone sold on the London market. Peter Carey still had the others, and young Neligan, as he said, wanted to get them. After he had run away he did not dare to get near the house again for some time, but at last he forced himself to do so to get what he wanted. Surely that is all simple and clear."

Holmes smiled.

"There is just one thing, Hopkins, and that is that it is really impossible. Have you tried to drive a harpoon through a body? No? My dear sir, you must really think of these small things. My friend, Watson, could tell you that I spent a whole morning trying to. It is no easy matter, you must have a strong and *practised* arm. But the harpoon was driven through Peter Carey with such force that it sank deep into the wall. Do you think that this young man could do that? Is he the man who had rum and water with Black Peter in the dead of the night? Was it his shadow that was seen on the curtain two nights before? No, no, Hopkins. It is another and stronger person for whom we must seek."

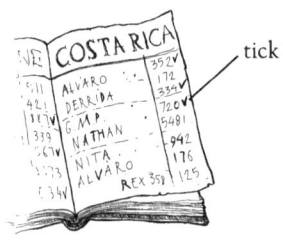

| *practised*, he has done it many times before

The detective's face had become longer and longer during Holmes' speech, but he would not give up his position.

"You must admit that Neligan was present that night, Mr. Holmes. The book will prove that. And, Mr. Holmes, I have laid my hand upon my man. As to this person of yours, where is he?"

"I think that he will soon be here," said Holmes. "And I think, Watson, that you would do well to put that

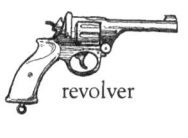

revolver where you can reach it." He rose, and laid a written paper on a side-table. "Now we are ready," he said.

There had been some talking outside, and now Mrs. Hudson opened the door to say that there were three men asking for Captain Basil.

"Show them in one by one," said Holmes.

The first who entered was a little man with red cheeks and white *side-whiskers*. Holmes had taken a letter from his pocket.

"What name?" he asked.

"James Lancaster."

"I am sorry, Lancaster, but the ship is full. Here is half a pound for your trouble. Just step into this room and wait there for a few minutes."

The second was a long man with thin hair and a rather

pale face. His name was Hugh Pattins. He also received half a pound and the order to wait in the other room.

The third was a big man with an angry *bull-dog* face, a mass of long hair and a beard, and two dark eyes shining
5 behind thick *eyebrows*. He stood before Holmes, turning his *cap* round in his hands.

"Your name?" asked Holmes.

"Patrick Cairns."

"*Harpooner*?""

10 "Yes, sir."

"Dundee, I suppose?"

"Yes, sir."

"What pay?"

"Eight pounds a month."

15 "Could you start at once?"

"As soon as I could get my things."

"Have you your papers?"

"Yes, sir." He took some papers from his pocket. Holmes looked them over and returned them.

20 "You are just the man I want," said he. "If you will write your name on the *agreement* there on the side-table the whole matter is all right."

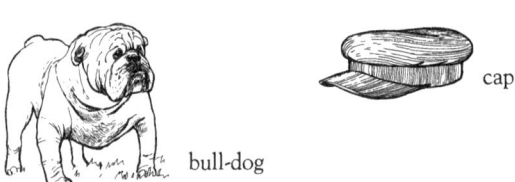

cap

bull-dog

eyebrow: see picture on page 39
harpooner, man who catches seals and whales by using a harpoon
agreement, paper saying that he agrees to work in the ship and get eight pounds a week for his work

The seaman walked across the room and took up the pen.

"Shall I write here?" he asked, bending over the table.

Holmes leaned over his shoulder and passed both hands over his neck.

"This will do," said he.

The next moment Holmes and the seaman were rolling on the floor together. He was a man so strong that, even with the *handcuffs* on his *wrists*, he would have killed my friend had Hopkins and I not helped him. Only when I pressed the revolver to his head did he understand that he had lost. We rose from the floor.

"I am really sorry, Hopkins," said Sherlock Holmes. "I am afraid that your egg is cold. You will enjoy the rest of your breakfast all the better, will you not, for the thought that you have brought our case to an end."

Stanley Hopkins was so surprised that he could not say anything.

"I don't know what to say, Mr. Holmes, he said at last, with a very red face. "It seems to me that I have been making a fool of myself from the beginning. I don't understand it. I see what you have done, but I don't know how you did it, or what it means."

"Well, well," said Holmes. "We all learn, and what you have learned this time is that you should never forget the alternative. You thought so much about young Neligan that you had no thought for Patrick Cairns, the real murderer of Peter Carey."

The voice of the seaman broke in on our talk.

"See here, mister," said he. "I'll say nothing to what you have done, but I would have you call things by their right names. You say I murdered Peter Carey; I say that I killed Peter Carey, and there is all the difference. Maybe you won't believe what I say. Maybe you think I'm just telling you a story."

"Not at all," said Holmes. "Let us hear what you have

| *handcuffs, wrist*: see picture on page 41

to say."

"It's soon told, and every word of it is true. I knew Black Peter, and when he pulled out his knife I ran a harpoon through him, for I knew that it was him or me. That's how he died. You can call it murder. But I would as soon be hanged as die with Black Peter's knife in my heart."

"How came you there?" asked Holmes.

"I'll tell you from the beginning. Just sit me up a little so I can speak easy. It was in '83 that it happened – August of that year. Peter Carey was captain of the SEA UNICORN, and I was harpooner. We were coming out of the ice on our way home, with a week's storm from the south, when we picked up a little yacht that had been blown north. There was one man on her – a *landsman*.

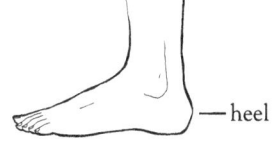

Well, we picked him up, this man, and he and the captain had some long talks in the cabin. The only thing we took off with him was one small box. So far as I know the man's name was never mentioned, and on the second night he disappeared as if he had never been. It was given out that he had fallen *overboard* in the heavy weather that we were having. Only one man knew what had happened to him, and that was me, for with my own eyes I saw the captain tip up his *heels* and

landsman, one who lives and works on land
overboard, into the sea

put him over the *rail* in the middle of a dark night, two days before we saw the Shetland lights."

"Well, I kept my knowledge to myself and waited to see what would come of it. When we got back to Scotland, nobody said anything about it, and nobody asked any questions. A short time after Peter Carey gave up the sea, and it was long years before I could find where he was. I guessed that he had put Neligan over the rail because of what was in that box, and that he ought to pay me well now for keeping my mouth shut."

"I found out where he was through a seaman that had seen him in London, and down I went to talk with him. The first night he was kind enough and was ready to give me what would make me free of the sea for life. We were to meet again two nights later. When I came, we sat down and we drank and we talked about old times, but the more he drank the less I liked the look on his face. I saw that harpoon on the wall, and I thought I might need it before I was through. Then at last he broke out at me with murder in his eyes and a great knife in his hands. He had not time to get it from the sheath before I had the harpoon through him. Heavens! what a yell he gave; and his face gets between me and my sleep. I stood there and I waited for a while; but all was quiet, so I took heart once more. I looked round, and there was the box on a shelf. I had as much right to it as Peter Carey, so I took it with me and left the house. Like a fool I left my tobacco-pouch on the table."

"Now I'll tell you the strangest part of the story. I had hardly got outside the house when I heard someone coming and sat down behind the bushes. A man came along, went into the cabin, gave a cry and ran away as fast as he could until he was out of sight. Who he was or what he wanted is more than I can tell. For my part, I walked ten miles, got on a train at Tunbridge Wells and so reached London."

"Well, when I came to examine the box I found there was no money in it, and nothing but papers that I would not dare to sell. I had no money, so when I saw in a newspaper that the shipping agent wanted harpooners, I went to him and he sent me here. That's all I know, and I say again that if I killed Black Peter, you ought to thank me."

"It is all very clear," said Holmes. "I think, Hopkins, that you should lose no time in taking Mr. Patrick Cairns to the police station."

"Mr. Holmes," said Hopkins, "I do not know how to thank you. Even now I do not understand how you came to this result."

"Only because I happened to get the right idea in the beginning. It is very possible that if I had known about this notebook, it might have led away my thoughts as it did yours. But all I heard pointed in one direction. The harpoon, the rum and water, the sealskin tobacco-pouch – all these pointed to a seaman, and one who had been a harpooner. I was sure that the initials P.C. upon the pouch were not those of Peter Carey as he smoked very little, and no pipe was found in his cabin. You remember that I asked if whisky and brandy were in the cabin. You said they were. How many landsmen are there who would drink rum when they could get whisky or brandy. Yes, I was certain it was a seaman."

"And how did you find him?"

"My dear sir, the problem had become a very simple one. If it were a seaman, it could only be a seaman who had been with him on the SEA UNICORN. So far as I could learn, he had sailed in no other ship. From Dundee I got the names of *the crew* of the SEA UNICORN in 1883. When I found Patrick Cairns among the harpooners, I had my man. I thought that he was probably in London and that he would like to leave the country for a time. I therefore went to the East End as Captain Basil, said that I wanted harpooners and that I would pay them

| *the crew*, the men who worked in the ship

well and this is the result."

"Wonderful!" cried Hopkins. "Wonderful."

"You must talk to young Neligan as soon as possible.

The box must be returned to him, but of course the securities which Peter Carey has sold are lost for ever.

There's the four-wheeler, Hopkins, and you can take your man away. If you want me later, my *address* and that of Watson will be somewhere in Norway – I shall write to you about it later."

| *address*, the street, house etc. where they will stay

Questions

Chapter 1.

1. Who was Stanley Hopkins?

2. Why did Black Peter call the small house his "cabin"?

3. How had Black Peter been killed?

4. What was in the notebook?

5. What were the initials on the tobacco-pouch?

Chapter 2.

1. What did the daughter say about her father?

2. What did Hopkins notice when he was going to open the door?

3. Why did Holmes want to be at the cabin at night?

Chapter 3.

1. Who came to the cabin?

2. Why did Mr. Neligan leave in his yacht?

3. Why did John Neligan want to see Black Peter?

Chapter 4.

1. Why was it impossible that John Neligan had killed Peter Carey?

2. Who was Patrick Cairns?

3. Why did Patrick Cairns kill Black Peter?

THE RED-HEADED LEAGUE

The Read-Headed *League*

1.

I had called upon my friend, Mr. Sherlock Holmes, one day in the *autumn* of last year, and found him talking to a very big, red-faced gentleman with *fiery*, red hair. I was about to leave when Holmes pulled me into the room and closed the door behind me.

"You could not have come at a better time, my dear Watson," he said.

"I was afraid you *were engaged*."

"So I am. Very much so."

"Then I can wait in the next room."

"Not at all. This gentleman, Mr. Wilson, has been my helper in many of my best cases, and I have no doubt that he will be of great use to me in yours also."

The gentleman half rose from his chair and bowed.

"Try the *settee*," said Holmes, sitting down in his *armchair*, and putting his fingers together. "I know, my dear Watson, that you share my love of all that is strange and outside everyday life. You have shown your interest for it by recording so many of my cases."

"Your cases have indeed been of the greatest interest to me," I said.

---

league, club; group of people, countries etc. working together
autumn, the time of year between summer and winter
fiery, like fire
were engaged, were talking to someone
settee, armchair: see picture on page 56

"Well, well," Holmes said. "Mr. Jabez Wilson here has been good enough to call upon me this morning, and to begin a story which promises to be one of the most interesting that I have listened to for some time. You
5 have heard me say that the strangest cases are very often the smaller *crimes*. As far as I have heard, it is impossible for me to say if the present case is a crime or not, but what has happened is certainly very strange. Perhaps, Mr. Wilson, you will begin your story again. I ask you
10 not only because my friend, Dr. Watson, has not heard the opening part, but also because the strange nature of your story makes me want to have everything from your own lips. I must say that in this case the facts are very strange indeed."
15 The man pulled a paper from the pocket of his *greatcoat*. As he looked at the *advertisements* in the paper on his knee, I took a good look at the man, and tried to see what I could learn about him.

settee

armchair

crime, killing another person is a crime
advertisement, if you want to make something known to other people, you put an advertisement in a newspaper

Our visitor had every mark of being a British *tradesman*, *fat* and slow. He had rather big, grey *trousers*, a not over-clean, black *frock-coat*, a brown *waistcoat*, a heavy Albert *chain*, and a bit of metal hanging down from it. An old *top-hat* and an old, brown greatcoat lay upon a chair beside him. Look as I would, there was nothing

tradesman, man who has a shop
fat, if you eat too much, you get fat

particular about the man except his red head.

Sherlock Holmes smiled when he saw what I was doing. "Beyond the facts that he has at some time been

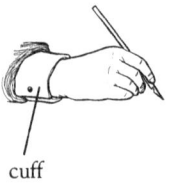
cuff

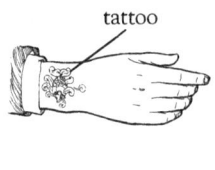
tattoo

a worker, that he takes *snuff*, that he has been in China,
5 and that he has done a lot of writing, I can see nothing else."

Mr. Jabez Wilson started up in his chair, with his hand upon the paper, but his eyes on my friend.

"How on earth did you know all that, Mr. Holmes?"
10 he asked. "How did you know, for example, that I have been a worker?"

"Your hands, my dear sir. Your right hand is quite a size larger than your left. You have worked with it."

"That's true. But the writing?"

15 "What else can it mean that your right *cuff* is so very *shiny* where it lies on the table when you write?"

"Well, but China?"

"The *tattoo* of the fish which you have above your right wrist could only have been done in China. I have
20 made a small study of tattoo marks, and have even

> *snuff*, something put up into the nose by some people instead of smoking
> *shiny*, it shines because he moved it on the table when he was writing

written a book about it. And when I see a *Chinese coin* hanging from your watch-chain, the matter becomes even more simple."

Mr. Jabez Wilson laughed heavily. "Well, I never!" said he. "I thought at first you had done something *clever*, but I see that there was nothing in it after all."

"I begin to think, Watson," said Holmes, "that I make a mistake in explaining. Can you not find the advertisement, Mr. Wilson?"

"Yes, I have got it now," he answered, with his thick, red finger half-way down the page. "Here it is. This is what began it all. You just read it for yourself, sir."

I took the paper from him and read as follows:

"TO THE RED-HEADED LEAGUE. – Because of the *will* of the *late* Ezekiah Hopkins, of Lebanon, Penn., U.S.A., there is now another position open which gives a member of the League the right to a *salary* of four pounds a week for purely *nominal services*. All red-headed men who are *sound* in body and mind and above the age of twenty-one years can get the position. *Apply* in

 coin

Chinese, from China
clever, quick in learning and understanding things
will, paper saying who is going to have his money after his death
late, not living any more
salary, money received for work
nominal services, work in name only, that is: little or no work
sound, not ill
apply, ask to be given

person on Monday, at eleven o'clock, to Duncan Ross, at the offices of the League, 7 Pope's Court, Fleet Street."

"What on earth does this mean?" I said, after I had read over the advertisement.

Holmes laughed in the way he did when he was pleased. "And now, Mr. Wilson, off you go, and tell us all about yourself, your family, and the effect which this advertisement had upon your business. You will first make a note, Doctor, of the paper and the date."

"It is THE MORNING CHRONICLE, of April 27, 1890. Just two months ago."

"Very good. Now, Mr. Wilson?"

"Well, it is just as I have been telling you, Mr. Sherlock Holmes," said Jabez Wilson. "I have a small *pawnbroker's* business at Coburg Square, near the City. It is not a very large affair, and of late years it has not done more than just give me enough. I used to keep two *assistants*, but now I only keep one, and I can only do that because he is willing to come for half pay, so as to learn the business."

"His name is Vincent Spaulding, and he's not young. It is hard to say his age. I should not wish a cleverer assistant, Mr. Holmes; and I know very well that he could get a better position, and *earn more* than what I am able to give him. But after all, if he is satisfied, why should I put ideas in his head?"

---

pawnbroker, if you want money you can get it at a pawnbroker's if you give him for example your watch. When you return the money you get your watch back.
assistants, men to help him in the shop
earn more, make more money

"Why, indeed? You must be pleased to have an assistant who comes under the full market price. It is not a usual thing today. I don't know that your assistant is not as strange as your advertisement."

"Oh, he has his *faults*, too," said Mr. Wilson. "Never was such a fellow for taking *photographs*. Running away with a *camera* when he ought to be working, and then going down to make his pictures. That is his greatest fault; but on the whole he is a good worker. There is nothing bad in him."

"He is still with you, I suppose?"

"Yes, sir, he and a girl of fourteen, who does a bit of simple cooking, and keeps the place clean – that's all I have in the house, for I am a *widower*, and never had any family. We live very quietly, sir, the three of us; and we keep a roof over our heads, and pay our *debts*, if we do nothing more."

"The first thing that troubled us was that advertisement. Spaulding, he came down into the office just this day eight weeks with this very paper in his hand, and he says:

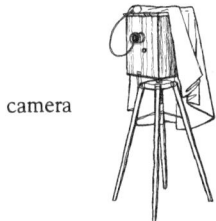

camera

---

faults, he is not always as good as he should be
photograph, picture taken with a camera
widower, man whose wife has died
debt, money you must pay to somebody else

"I wish, Mr. Wilson, that I was a red-headed man."

"Why that?" I ask.

"Why," says he, "here's another position in the League of the Red-Headed Men. It's worth quite a lot of money to any man who gets it, and I understand that there are more positions than there are men, so that they don't know what to do with the money. If my hair would only change colour!"

"Why, what is it, then," I asked. "You see, Mr. Holmes, I am a very stay-at-home man, and, as my business came to me instead of my having to go to it, I was often weeks on end without going out. In that way I didn't know much of what was going on outside, and I was always glad of a bit of news."

"Have you never heard of the League of the Red-Headed Men?" he asked, with his eyes open.

"Never."

"Why, I wonder at that, for you can get one of the positions yourself."

"And what are they worth?" I asked.

"Oh, only some hundred pounds a year, but there is little work."

"Well, you can easily think that that made me listen, for the business has not been over good for some years, and some hundred a year would have been very good."

"Tell me all about it," said I.

"Well," said he, showing me the advertisement, "you can see for yourself that the League has a *vacancy*, and there is the *address* where you should apply if you want to know more about it. As far as I can make out, the League

vacancy, position which someone can have
address, the street, house etc. where the office is.

was started by a rich American, Ezekiah Hopkins, who was very strange in his ways. He was himself red-headed, and it was his wish to help all red-headed men; so, when he died, it was found that he had left his money in the hands of *trustees*, with orders that they were to help men 5
whose hair is of that colour to easy and pleasant work.

trustees, persons who were to see to it that the money was given to red-headed men only

From all I hear it is excellent pay and very little to do."

"But," said I, "there would be millions of red-headed men who would apply."

"Not so many as you might think," he answered. "You see, it is only Londoners who can apply and only men over 21. This American had started from London when he was young, and he wanted to do something for the old town. Then , again, I have heard it is no use applying if one's hair is light red, or dark red, or anything but real, fiery red. Now, if you cared to apply, you would just walk in; but perhaps it would hardly be worth your while to put yourself out of the way for a few hundred pounds."

"Now, it is a fact, gentlemen, as you may see for yourselves, that my hair is of a very full and rich colour, so that it seemed to me that I stood as good a chance as any man that I had ever seen. Vincent Spaulding seemed to know so much about it that I thought it might be good to have him with me, so I just ordered him to close the shop for the day and to come right away with me. He was glad to have a *holiday*, so we shut the business up and started off for the address that was given us in the advertisement."

"I never hope to see such a sight again, Mr. Holmes. From north, south, east, and west every man who had a little red in his hair had come to the City to answer the advertisement. Fleet Street was full of red-headed people. I should not have thought that there were so many in the whole country as were brought together by that single advertisement. When I saw how many were waiting, I would have given it up, but Spaulding would not hear of it. How he did it I don't know, but

| *holiday*, you don't work on a holiday

he got me through the *crowd* and right up to the steps which led to the office. There was a double stream there, some going up in hope, and some coming back *dejected*; but we got in, and soon found ourselves in the office."

crowd, many people together
dejected, looking sad because they had not got the position

"Your experience has been a most interesting one," said Holmes, as his client stopped to take a *pinch* of snuff. "Please continue your interesting story."

"There was nothing in the office but some chairs and a table, behind which sat a small man whose hair was even redder than mine. He said a few words to each man as he came up, and then he always found some fault in them and sent them away. Getting a vacancy did not seem to be such a very easy matter after all. However, when our turn came, the little man was more interested in me than in any of the others, and he closed the door as we entered, so that he might have a private word with us.

"This is Mr. Jabez Wilson," said my assistant, "and he wants to fill a vacancy in the League."

"And he is very well *suited for* it," the other answered. "I cannot remember when I have seen anything so fine," he said, looking at my hair. Then suddenly he came forward, took my hair in both his hands and pulled until I cried with the pain. "There is water in your eyes," said he, "I think that all is as it should be. But we have to act with care." He stepped over to the window, and shouted through it at the top of his voice that the vacancy was filled. The people all walked away in different directions until there was not a red head to be seen except my own and that of the little man.

"My name," said he, "is Mr. Duncan Ross, and I am myself one of *the pensioners*. Are you a married man, Mr. Wilson? Have you a family?"

---

pinch, as much as you can take with two fingers
suited for, has the right qualities
the pensioners, those who get money

I answered that I had not.

"Dear me!" he said, "that is very serious indeed! I am sorry to hear you say that. The money was, of course, for *increasing* the number of red-heads as well as for helping them. It is very sad that you should be a *bachelor*."

"I was sorry to hear this, Mr. Holmes, for I thought that I was not to have the vacancy after all; but after thinking it over for a few minutes, he said that it would be all right."

"In the case of another," said he, "he would not have got the vacancy. But we can't refuse a man with such a head of hair as yours. When shall you be able to enter upon your new duties?"

"Well, it is a bit difficult, for I have a business already," said I.

"Oh, never mind about that, Mr. Wilson!" said Vincent Spaulding. "I shall be able to look after that for you."

"What would be the hours?" I asked.

"Ten to two."

Now a pawnbroker's business is mostly done of an evening, Mr. Holmes, and mostly Thursday and Friday evening, which is just before pay-day. So it would suit me very well to make a little money in the mornings. I knew that my assistant was a good man, and that he would see to anything that turned up.

"That would suit me very well," said I. "And the pay?"

"Is four pounds a week."

"And the work?"

"Is purely nominal."

---

increase, make or become greater in number
bachelor, man who has not married

"What do you call purely nominal?"

"Well, you have to be in the office, or at least in the building the whole time. If you leave, you will lose your whole position for ever."

"It is only four hours a day, and I should not think of leaving," said I. "But the work?"

"Is to *copy out* the ENCYCLOPAEDIA BRITANNICA. There is the first book in that *press*. You must find your own *ink* and pens, but we give you this table and chair. Will you be ready tomorrow?"

"Certainly," I answered.

"Then good-bye, Mr. Wilson, and let me *congratulate* you on the important position which you have got." He showed me out of the room, and I went home with my assistant, hardly knowing what to say or do, I was so happy.

"Well, I thought over the matter all day, and by evening I was unhappy again; for I thought that the whole affair was some great *joke*, though what its object might be I could not guess. I could not believe that anyone would pay so much money for doing anything so simple as copying out the ENCYCLOPAEDIA BRITANNICA, and by bedtime I had decided to give it up. However, in the morning I made up my mind to have a look at it after all, so I bought a *bottle* of ink, and with a pen and some paper I started off for Pope's Court.

---

copy out, write everything which is in the book
encyclopaedia, book (or books) with articles in ABC order about everything
congratulate, say to someone that you are pleased with his succes
joke, something done to make people laugh at him

"Well, to my surprise everything was as right as possible. The table was set out ready for me, and Mr. Duncan Ross was there to see that I got to work. He started me off upon the letter A, and then he left me; but he would drop in from time to time to see that all was right with me. At two o'clock he said good-bye to me, said that he was pleased with the number of pages that I had written, and shut the door of the office after me."

"This went on day after day, Mr. Holmes, and on Saturday he came in and gave me four pounds for my

week's work. It was the same the next week, and the same the week after. Every morning I was there at ten, and every afternoon I left at two. After some time Mr. Duncan Ross took to coming in only once of a morning, and then, after some weeks, he did not come in at all. Still, of course, I did not dare to leave the room for a moment, for I was not sure when he might come, and the position was such a good one, and suited me so well that I did not want to lose it."

"Eight weeks passed away like this, and I had written nearly all the A's and hoped that I might pass on to the

B's before very long. It cost me something in paper, and I had nearly filled a *shelf* with my writings. And then suddenly the whole business came to an end."

shelf

"To an end?"

"Yes, sir, and no later than this morning. I went to my work as usual at ten o'clock, but the door was shut and *locked*, and there was a little piece of paper on it. Here it is, and you can read for yourself."

He held up a piece of white paper. It read:

THE RED-HEADED LEAGUE *IS DISSOLVED*.
OCT. 9, 1890

Sherlock Holmes and I looked at it. Then we both began to laugh.

"I cannot see that there is anything very *funny*," cried our *client*. "If you can do nothing better than laugh at

> *locked*, it could not open
> *is dissolved*, is no more
> *funny*, if something is funny, you will laugh at it
> *client*, Holmes's clients are the people who come to him for help

me, I can go to someone else."

"No, no," cried Holmes, pushing him back into the chair, from which he had half risen. "I really wouldn't miss your case for the world. It is so *unusual*. But there

| *unusual*, strange or surprising

is something just a little funny about it. What steps did you take when you found it upon the door?"

"I did not know what to do. Then I called at the offices round, but none of them seemed to know anything about it. At last I went to the *landlord* and asked him if he could tell me what had become of the Red-Headed League. He said that he had never heard of any such body. Then I asked him who Mr. Duncan Ross was. He answered that the name was new to him.

"Well," said I, "the gentleman at No. 4."

"What, the red-headed man?"

"Yes."

"Oh," said he, "his name was William Morris. He was a *lawyer*, and was using my room until his own office was ready. He moved out yesterday."

"Where could I find him?"

"Oh, at his new office. He did tell me the address. Yes, 17 King Edward Street, near St. Paul's."

"I started off, Mr. Holmes, but when I got to that address it was a shop, and no one in it had ever heard of either Mr. William Morris, or Mr. Duncan Ross."

"And what did you do then?" asked Holmes.

"I went home and talked with my assistant. But he could not help me in any way. He could only say that if I waited, I should hear by post. But that was not quite good enough, Mr. Holmes. I did not wish to lose such a place, so, as I had heard that you were good enough to help poor people who were in need of help, I came right away to you."

"And you did very wisely," said Holmes. "Your case is

landlord, the man who owned the house
lawyer, person who has studied law

a very strange one, and I shall be happy to look into it. From what you have told me, I think that it is possible that more serious things hang from it than might at first sight appear."

"Serious enough!" said Mr. Jabez Wilson. "Why, I have lost four pounds a week."

"As to yourself," said Holmes, "I understand that you are richer by some thirty pounds, to say nothing of the knowledge which you have got on everything which comes under the letter A. You did not lose anything by them."

"No, sir. But I want to find out about them, and who they are, and what their object was in playing this joke – if it was a joke – upon me. It was a rather *expensive* joke for them, for it cost them two-and-thirty pounds."

"We shall try to clear up these points for you. And, first, one or two questions, Mr. Wilson. This assistant of yours, who first told you about the advertisement – how long had he been with you?"

"About a month then."

"How did he come?"

"In answer to an advertisement."

"Was he the only one who applied?"

"No, there were twelve."

"Why did you pick him?"

"Because he would come *cheap*."

"At half wages, in fact."

"Yes."

"What is he like, this Vincent Spaulding?"

"Small, quite strong, very quick in his ways, no hair on

expensive, costing much money
cheap, costing little money

his face, though he's not short of thirty. He has a white *spot* on his *forehead*."

"I thought as much," said he. "Have you ever observed if his ears are *pierced* for ear-rings?"
5 "Yes, sir. He told me that it had been done when he was a boy."
"Hum!" said Holmes, sitting for a while in deep thought. "He is still with you?"
"Oh, yes, sir; I have only just left him."
10 "And has he looked after your business when you were not there?"
"Certainly, sir. There's never very much to do of a morning."
"That will do, Mr. Wilson. I shall be happy to talk to
15 you again in a day or two. Today is Saturday, and I hope that by Monday I can tell you what it is all about."

| *pierced*, something had been put through them to make holes

2.

"Well, Watson," said Holmes when Mr. Wilson had left us, "what do you make of it all?"

"I make nothing of it," I answered. "It is a very strange business."

"Usually," said Holmes, "the stranger a thing seems to

be, the less difficult it is. But I must be quick over this matter."

"What are you going to do then?" I asked.

"To smoke," he answered. "It is quite a three-*pipe* problem, and I ask you not to speak to me for fifty minutes." He sat down in his chair with his black pipe in his mouth.

I thought that he had dropped asleep, and was indeed sleeping myself, when he suddenly sprang out of his chair like a man who had made up his mind and put his pipe down on the table.

"Sarasate plays at the St. James's Hall this afternoon," he said. "What do you think, Watson?"

"I have nothing to do today."

"Then put on your hat, and come. I am going through the City first, and we can have some lunch on the way. He is going to play some very good music. Come along!"

We travelled by train as far as Aldersgate; and a short walk took us to Saxe-Coburg Square, the scene of the story which we had listened to in the morning. It was a little place with four lines of small, dirty-looking houses. A Brown *board* with "JABEZ WILSON" in white letters upon a corner house told us that this was the place where our red-headed client carried on his business. Sherlock Holmes stopped in front of it and looked it all over. Then he walked slowly up the street and then down again to the corner, still looking at the houses. At last he returned to the pawnbroker's, beat upon the *pavement* two or three times with his stick, and then went up to the door and knocked. It was opened at once by a young fellow who asked him to step in.

| *pipe*: see picture on page 75

"Thank you," said Holmes, "I only wished to ask you how you would go from here to the Strand."

"First right, second left," answered the assistant at once, closing the door.

"Clever fellow, that," observed Holmes as we walked away. "He is, I think, the fourth cleverest man in London, and I am not sure that he is not the third. I have known something of him before."

"Clearly," said I, "Mr. Wilson's assistant counts for a great deal in this *mystery* of the Red-Headed League. I am sure that you asked your way only in order that you might see him."

"Not him."

"What then?"

"The knees of his trousers."

"And what did you see?"

"What I expected to see."

"Why did you beat the pavement?"

"My dear Doctor, this is a time for *observation*, not for talk. We know something about Saxe-Cobourg Square. Let us now have a look at the streets which lie behind it."

The street in which we found ourselves as we turned round the corner was very different from Saxe-Coburg Square. The pavements were black with people, and there were a lot of fine shops and many big business offices.

"Let me see," said Holmes, standing at the corner, and looking along the line of shops, "I should like just to remember the order of the houses here. I like to have a good knowledge of London. And now, Doctor, we've done our work, so it's time we had some play. Some lunch, and then off to music land, where there are no red-headed clients to trouble us with their questions."

mystery, something which is very strange and difficult to explain
observation, looking around

My friend was himself a good *musician*. All the afternoon he sat listening happily waving his long thin fingers in time to the music.

| *musician*, person who plays music

3.

"You want to go home, no doubt, Doctor," said Holmes as we came out from St. James's Hall.

"Yes, it would be as well."

"And I have some business to do which will take some hours. This business at Coburg Square is serious."

"Why serious?"

"They are planning some great crime. I believe that we shall be in time to stop them. But today being Saturday makes matters rather difficult. I shall want your help tonight."

"At what time?"

"Ten will be early enough."

"I shall be at Baker Street at ten."

"Very well. And, I say, Doctor! kindly put your *revolver* in your pocket!" He waved his hand, turned round and walked away.

I believe that I am as clever as my neighbours, but I was always filled with a sense of being a fool when I was with Sherlock Holmes. Here I had heard what he had heard, I had seen what he had seen, and yet from his words it was clear that he saw not only what had happened, but what was about to happen, while the whole business was still a mystery to me. As I went home to my house in Kensington, I thought over it all, from the strange story of the red-headed man who copied out the ENCYCLOPAEDIA down to the visit to Saxe-Coburg Square, and the words with which he had left me. What was this nightly affair, and why should I take my revolver

| *revolver*: see picture on page 39

hansom

with me. Where were we going, and what were we to do? I tried to think it out, but gave it up, and set the matter aside until night.

It was a quarter past nine when I started from home and made my way across the Park, and so through Oxford Street to Baker Street. Two *hansoms* were standing at the door, and, as I entered the house, I heard the sound of voices from above. When I entered his room, I found Holmes talking to two men, one of whom I recognized as Peter Jones, the *police* officer; while the other was long, thin, sad-faced man, with a very shiny hat and a frock-coat.

"Ha! our party is complete," said Holmes. "Watson, I think you know Mr. Jones, of *Scotland Yard*? And this is

police: see picture on page 13
Scotland Yard, the London police

Mr. Merryweather, who is to be with us tonight."

"We are working *in couples* again, Doctor, you see," said Jones. "Our friend here is a wonderful man for starting a *chase*. All he wants is an old dog to help him do the *running down*."

goose

"I hope a wild *goose* may not prove to be at the end of the chase," observed Mr. Merryweather sadly.

"You may believe in Mr. Holmes, sir," said the police agent. "He has his own little *methods*, which are, if he won't mind me saying so, just a little strange, but he has the making of a *detective* in him. It is not too much to say that two or three times, as in the Sholto mystery, he has been more nearly right than the police."

"Oh, if you say so, Mr. Jones, it is all right!" said Mr. Merryweather. "Still, I must say that I miss my bridge.

---

in couples, two and two
chase, attempt to catch someone. A wild-goose chase: chasing someone you cannot find
run someone down, find someone by looking for him
method, way of doing things
detective, person, often a policeman, whose job it is to find and catch people who have for example stolen something or killed someone

It is the first Saturday night for seven-and-twenty years that I have not played bridge."

"I think you will find," said Sherlock Holmes, "that you will play for more money tonight than you have ever done yet. For you, Mr. Merryweather, it will be some thirty thousand pounds; and for you, Jones, it will be the man you wish to lay your hands on."

"John Clay, the *murderer* and *thief*. He is a young man, Mr. Merryweather, but I would rather have my hands on him than on any *criminal* in London. He is a strange man, is young John Clay. He has a good head, and though we meet signs of him at every turn, we never know where to find the man himself. I have been chasing him for years, and have never set eyes on him yet."

"I hope you will tonight. I've had one or two little turns also with Mr. John Clay, and I agree with you that he is very clever. It is past ten, however, and quite time that we started. If you will take the first hansom, Watson and I will follow in the second."

Sherlock Holmes did not talk much during the long drive. He lay back in the hansom *humming* the music which he had heard in the afternoon. We came through an endless number of small gas-lit streets until we came into Farringdon Street.

"We are close there now," my friend said. "This fellow, Merryweather, is a bank manager and personally interested in the matter. I thought it as well to have

---

murderer, person who has killed someone
thief, person who steals from other people
criminal, a thief and a murderer are criminals
hum, sing without moving the lips

Jones with us also. He is not a bad fellow, though a complete fool as a detective. Here we are, and they are waiting for us."

We had reached the same *crowded* street in which we
5 had found ourselves in the morning. We got out of the

| *crowded*, there were many people

hansoms, and, following Mr. Merryweather, we passed down a narrow street, and through a side door, which he opened for us. Within there was a small *corridor*, which ended in a heavy iron gate. This also was opened, and we went down some stone steps, which ended at another big gate. Mr. Merryweather stopped to light a *lantern*, and then led us down a dark passage, and so, after opening a third door, into a very big room, which was filled with *crates* and boxes.

"Nobody can get in from above," said Holmes as he held up the lantern and looked about him.

"Nor can anyone get in through the floor," said Mr. Merryweather, striking his stick upon the *flagstones* which lined the floor. "Why, dear me, it sounds quite *hollow!*" he cried, looking up in surprise.

"I must really ask you to be a little more quiet," said Holmes. "May I ask you to have the goodness to sit down upon one of those boxes and not say anything?"

Mr. Merryweather sat down on a crate while Holmes fell upon his knees upon the floor, and, with the lantern and a *magnifying lens*, began to examine the lines between the flagstones. A few seconds were enough to satisfy him, for he rose again and put his lens in his pocket.

"We have at least an hour before us," he said, "for they can hardly take any steps until the good pawnbroker is in bed. Then they will not lose a minute, for the sooner they do their work, the longer time they have to get away. We are now, Doctor – as no doubt

---

corridor, long, narrow room inside a building with doors and rooms on one or both sides
hollow, as if there was nothing under the flagstones
magnifying lens: see picture on page 24

you have guessed – in the *cellar* of the City branch of one of the biggest London banks. Mr. Merryweather will explain to you that there are reasons why the more *daring* criminals of London should be very interested in this cellar just now."

"It is our French gold," *whispered* the director. "We have heard that an attempt might be made to steal it."

"Your French gold?"

"Yes. We *borrowed* some months ago thirty thousand *napoleons* from the Bank of France. It has become known that this money is still lying in our cellar. In the crate upon which I sit are two thousand napoleons."

"And now it is time that we make our little plans," observed Holmes. "I expect that within an hour matters will come to a head. I think, Mr. Merryweather, that we must put that light out."

"And sit in the dark?"

"I am afraid so. These are daring men, and they may *do* us some *harm*. I shall stand behind this crate and you may hide behind those. If they fire, Watson, shoot them down."

I placed the revolver on the top of the crate behind which I sat. Holmes put out the light, and the room was completely dark.

"They have but one way to get out," whispered Holmes. "That is back through the house into Saxe-Coburg

---

cellar, underground room
daring, ready to do dangerous things
whisper, talk in a very low voice
borrowed, got money which they must pay back
napoleon, a French gold coin = twenty francs
do harm, hurt

Square. I hope that you have done what I asked you, Jones?"

"I have three men waiting at the front door."

"Then we have stopped all the holes. And now we must be silent and wait."

What a time it seemed! It was but an hour and a quarter, yet it appeared to me that the night must have almost gone and the sun be rising above us. My legs were *stiff*, for I feared to change my position. From where I was sitting I could look over the crate in the direction of the floor. Suddenly I saw a little light.

At first it was but a little yellow spot on the stone floor. Then it became a yellow line, and then a hole seemed to open and a hand appeared, a white hand, almost like a woman's, which felt about in the centre of the light. For a minute or more the hand, with its moving fingers, was there on the floor. Then it was gone as suddenly as it had appeared, and all was dark again except a single spot of light, which marked a small hole between the flags.

Then one of the flags turned over upon its side and left a big hole through which came the light of a lantern. Over the edge appeared a *boyish* face, which looked about it, and then, with a hand on either side of the opening, *drew* itself up until one knee rested upon the edge. In another moment he stood at the side of the hole, and after him came another man, small

---

stiff, he could not move his legs because he had been sitting in the same position for a long time
boyish, like a boy
drew, from draw (draw, drew, drawn)

like himself, with a *pale* face and a very red hair.

"It's all clear," he whispered. "Have you the *chisel* and the bags? Great Scott! Get away, Archie, get away!"

Sherlock Holmes had sprung out and taken the man by the *collar*. The other got away through the hole.

The man pointed a revolver at us, but Holmes's stick came down on the man's hand, and the revolver fell upon the floor.

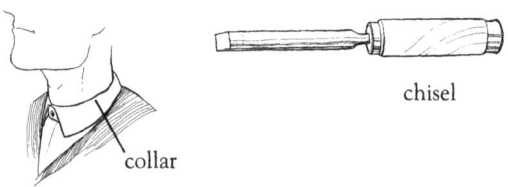

collar

chisel

"It's no use, John Clay," said Holmes quietly; "you have no chance at all."

"So I see," said the other, very cool. "I guess that my friend is all right."

"There are three men waiting for him at the door," said Holmes.

"Oh, indeed. You seem to have done the thing very completely. I must *compliment* you."

"And I you," Holmes answered. "Your red-headed idea was very new and very clever."

"You'll see your friend again soon," said Jones. "He's quicker at getting down holes than I am. Just hold out your hands while I put on the *handcuffs*."

> *pale*, (of a person's face) having little colour
> *compliment*, tell someone that you think he has done well
> *handcuffs*: see picture on page 41

"I ask you not to touch me with your dirty hands," said our *prisoner*. "You may not know that I have *royal* blood in me. Have the goodness also when you talk to me always to say "sir" and "please.""

"All right," said Jones with a laugh. "Well, would you

prisoner, criminal taken by the police
royal, belonging to the family of a king or queen

please, sir, go up into the street where we can get a hansom to carry your highness to the police station."

"That's better," said John Clay. He made a bow to the three of us, and walked quietly off with the detective.

"Really, Mr. Holmes," said Mr. Merryweather as we followed them from the cellar, I do not know how the bank can thank you or pay you. There is no doubt that you have discovered and stopped in the cleverest manner one of the most serious attempts to *rob* the bank that I have ever heard about."

"I have been at some small *expense* over this matter, which I shall expect the bank to pay me, but beyond that I am paid well enough by having had an unusual *adventure*, and by hearing the very interesting story of the Red-Headed League."

---

rob, take things of great value which belongs to someone else
expense, he had had to spend some money
adventure, strange, sometimes dangerous happening

4.

"You see, Watson," Holmes explained in the early hours of the morning, as we sat over a drink in Baker Street, "it was perfectly clear from the first that the only possible object of this rather unusual business of the advertisement of the League and the copying of the ENCYCLOPAEDIA, must be to get this pawnbroker out of the way for a number of hours every day. It was a strange way of doing it, but really it would be difficult to suggest a better one. The method was no doubt suggested to Clay's clever mind by the colour of the pawnbroker's hair. The four pounds a week was so much that it would draw him, and what was it to them who were playing for thousands? They put in the advertisement; one *rogue* has the office, the other rogue makes the man apply for it, and they are sure that he is away every morning in the week. From the time that I heard of the assistant having come for half-wages, it was clear to me that he had some reason for becoming the pawnbroker's assistant."

"But how could you guess why?"

"The man's business was a small one, and there was nothing in the house which could explain that they prepared themselves so well and were ready to spend so much money. It must then be something out of the house. I thought of the assistant's interest in photography and his going down into the cellar to make the pictures. The cellar! There it was! Then I tried to find out who this assistant was, and I found that I had to

| *rogue*, bad person

deal with one of the coolest and most daring criminals in London. He was doing something in the cellar – something which took many hours a day for months. What could it be, once more? I could think of nothing, except that he was running a *tunnel* to some other building.

"So far I had got when we went to visit the place. I surprised you by beating upon the pavement with my stick. I wanted to be sure whether the cellar was in front or behind. It was not in front. Then I knocked at the door, and, as I hoped, the assistant answered it. I hardly looked at his face. His knees were what I wished to see. You must yourself have seen how they looked. They spoke of those hours of making the tunnel. The only point was now what they were making it for. I walked round the corner, saw that the City Bank was behind our friend's house, and felt that I had found an answer to my question. When you went home from St. James's Hall, I called upon Scotland Yard and upon the director of the bank, with the result that you have seen."

"And how could you tell that they would make their attempt tonight?" I asked.

"Well, when they closed their League office that was a sign that they cared no longer about Mr. Jabez Wilson; in other words that they had completed their tunnel. But it was important that they should use it soon, as it might be discovered, or the money might be taken away. Saturday would suit them better than any other day as it would give them two days to get away. For all these reasons I expected them to come tonight."

"You thought it out beautifully," I said.

"It gave me something to think about," he answered. "And I am happy for that. I try as hard as I can to *escape* from the *commonplaces* of life. These little problems help me to do so.

---

escape, get away from, not have to deal with
commonplaces, ordinary or usual happenings

Questions

Chapter 1.

1. Why had Mr. Jabez Wilson come to see Holmes?

2. Who were going to have Mr. Ezekiah Hopkin's money after him?

3. How did Mr. Wilson learn about the Red-Headed League?

4. What did Mr. Wilson do in the office of the League?

Chapter 2.

1. Where did Holmes and Watson go before they went to St. James's Hall?

2. Who did Holmes speak to at the pawnbroker's shop?

3. Where did Holmes and Watson go when they had seen enough of Coburg Square?

Chapter 3.

1. Who were at Baker Street in the evening?

2. Who was Mr. Jones? And Mr. Merryweather?

3. How did they get to the bank?

4. Where did Mr. Merryweather take them?

5. How did John Clay get into the cellar?

6. What did John Clay and his friend want in the cellar?

Chapter 4.

1. Why had John Clay put the advertisement about the Red-Headed League in the paper?

2. Who was Vincent Spaulding?

3. Why did Vincent Spaulding say that he was interested in photography?

www.easyreaders.eu

EASY READERS *Denmark*
ERNST KLETT SPRACHEN *Germany*
ARCOBALENO *Spain*
LIBER *Sweden*
PRACTICUM EDUCATIEF BV. *Holland*
EUROPEAN SCHOOLBOOKS PUBLISHING LTD. *UK and Eire*
WYDAWNICTWO LEKTORKLETT *Poland*
KLETT KIADO KFT. *Hungary*
NÜANS PUBLISHING *Turkey*
ALLECTO LTD. *Estonia*
EMC CORP. *USA*

This edition has been abridged and simplified to provide graduated reading exercises for students of English. Vocabulary and sentence structures have been selected because of their high frequency and practical value to the learner.
Words which are difficult to understand in context or fall out of the EASY READER frequency modules are explained by footnotes in simple English or by illustrations.
EASY READERS are suitable for use in schools, for home study, or simply for reading enjoyment. See the complete list of titles on the inside cover.
EASY READERS are also available in German, French, Spanish, Italian and Russian.

EASY READER TITLES NOW AVAILABLE:
Sir Arthur Conan Doyle: The Red Circle (A)
Sir Arthur Conan Doyle: The Speckled Band (A)
Lois Lowry: Number the Stars (A)
R. L. Stine: Stay Out of the Basement (A)
R. L. Stevenson: The Bottle Imp (A)
Oscar Wilde: The Canterville Ghost (A)
Oscar Wilde: The Canterville Ghost, dramatized version (A)
Enid Blyton: Five on a Treasure Island (B)
Roald Dahl: The Way up to Heaven and Other Stories (B)
Sir Arthur Conan Doyle: Black Peter - The Red-Headed League (B)
Lois Duncan: I know what you did last Summer (B)
Lois Duncan: Killing Mr. Griffin (B)
James Herriot: If Only They Could Talk (B)
Colin Higgins: Harold and Maude (B)
S.E. Hinton: The Outsiders (B)
Jerome K. Jerome: Three Men in a Boat (B)
Ira Levin: The Stepford Wives (B)
Pat Lowe: The Girl with No Name (B)
Brian Moore: Lies of Silence (B)
R. L. Stine: Fear Street: The Perfect Date (B)
Mark Twain: Tom Sawyer (B)
Oscar Wilde: The Happy Prince (B)
Richard Wright: Black Boy (B)
Karen Blixen: Out of Africa (C)
Tim Bowler: Storm Catchers (C)
Roald Dahl: Edward the Conqueror and Other Stories (C)
Charles Dickens: A Christmas Carol (C)
Sir Arthur Conan Doyle: The Hound of the Baskervilles (C)
Graham Greene: The Third Man (C)
James Heneghan: Safe House (C)
S.E. Hinton: Tex (C)
Ira Levin: Rosemary's Baby (C)
James Moloney: Gracey (C)
Celia Rees: Witch Child (C)
Mary Shelley: Frankenstein (C)
Alexander McCall Smith: Tears of the Giraffe (C)
R. L. Stevenson: Treasure Island (C)
Bram Stoker: Dracula (C)
Oscar Wilde: The Picture of Dorian Gray (C)
F. Scott Fitzgerald: The Great Gatsby (D)
Alan Sillitoe: The Loneliness of the Long Distance Runner (D)
R. L. Stevenson: Dr. Jekyll and Mr. Hyde (D)
Kurt Vonnegut: Slaughterhouse-Five (D)

ADULT:
Peter James: The Perfect Murder (B)
Stephen Speight: Doomed to Die (B)
Stephen Speight: Swindled (B)
Minette Walters: Chickenfeed (C)